To: MaryBeth
From Jan

Happy Birthday
2003

*It's the little things which
keep the world shining —
little beams by day and
little twinkles by night.*

— Leroy Brownlow

Simple Joys

A Reminder to Slow Down and Enjoy the Little Things in Life

A Blue Mountain Arts® Collection
Edited by Diane Mastromarino

Blue Mountain Press ™
Boulder, Colorado

Library of Congress Catalog Card Number: 2003009864
ISBN: 0-88396-766-9

ACKNOWLEDGMENTS appear on page 64.

Certain trademarks are used under license.

Manufactured in the United States of America.
First Printing: 2003

 This book is printed on recycled paper.

This book is printed on fine quality, laid embossed, 80 lb. paper. This paper has been specially produced to be acid free (neutral pH) and contains no groundwood or unbleached pulp. It conforms with all the requirements of the American National Standards Institute, Inc., so as to ensure that this book will last and be enjoyed by future generations.

Library of Congress Cataloging-in-Publication Data

Simple joys : a reminder to slow down and enjoy the little things in life / edited by Diane Mastromarino.
    p. cm.
  ISBN 0-88396-766-9 (pbk. : alk. paper)
  1. Conduct of life. I. Mastromarino, Diane, 1978-

  BF637.C5S5443 2003
  170'.44--dc21

2003009864
CIP

Blue Mountain Arts, Inc.

P.O. Box 4549, Boulder, Colorado 80306

Contents

(Authors listed in order of first appearance)

Leroy Brownlow

Donna Fargo

Nancye Sims

Douglas Pagels

Susan Polis Schutz

Suzanne Willis Zoglio, Ph.D.

Sarah Ban Breathnach

Maya Angelou

Sir J. Lubbock

Wilferd A. Peterson

Hamlin Garland

Max Ehrmann

Ruth Stout

Henri Amiel

Judy Ford

John Muir

Jonathan Kramer, Ph.D., and
    Diane Dunaway Kramer

Victoria Moran

Melody Beattie

Helen Keller

Brian Luke Seaward, Ph.D.

Morrie Schwartz

Ruth Fishel

Helen Lowrie Marshall

Ben Daniels

Emmet Fox

Mother Teresa

Suzanne Somers

Deana Marino

Mitch Finley

Ashley Rice

Elle Mastro

Joseph Campbell

Anne Morrow Lindbergh

Jenifer Nostrand

Jacqueline Schiff

Susan Mah

Francis Thompson

Josh Billings

George Gordon, Lord Byron

Elizabeth Kaeton

Linda Ann McConnell

Andrea Van Steenhouse, Ph.D.

Elaine St. James

Rochelle Lynn Holt

Vickie M. Worsham

Maryanne Hannan

Phylis Clay Sparks

Jackie Olson

Acknowledgments

Make Every Day Special

Make every day a day to celebrate life and be thankful. Take time to pull yourself away from all the noise and just look around you.

Take inventory. Appreciate those who have enhanced the quality of your life, and remember that they have been a gift to you. Also remember that you're a gift to them, too.

Be grateful for the choices you've made, both good and bad. Accept your mistakes; you can't change them anyway. Appreciate yourself and your own uniqueness.

Go outside and look at the sky. Soak in the atmosphere. Enjoy the colors of the landscape. Feel the textures of every place you are that you're thankful for. Smile at the world. Don't allow any negative feelings to creep into your consciousness. Feel the power of your own acceptance. Put a positive spin on every thought you have.

Make every day special. Own it. Enjoy it. Bask in the glory of life. Appreciate the gift of your own life.

— Donna Fargo

SLOW DOWN AND ENJOY EACH DAY

Don't run through life so fast that you forget not only where you've been but also where you're going. Life is not a race, but a journey to be savored each step of the way.

— Nancye Sims

See each day as a new opportunity to do the things that are important to you: the things that keep you healthy, happy, and safe from any harm. Every day you have a chance to fail or excel, to see circumstances as obstacles or challenges. Always leave room for intuition, but make every choice count.

— Donna Fargo

Let the day be carefree. Let it be as happy as a carnival and as much fun as a kaleidoscope. Keep all your options open. (If you can't quite decide between double-dutch chocolate OR poppy-seed cake with raspberry filling... have them both!)

Live to the fullest, and make each day count. Don't let the important things go unsaid. Have simple pleasures in this complex world. Be a joyous spirit and a sensitive soul. Take those long walks that would love to be taken. Explore those sunlit paths that would love to oblige. Don't just have minutes in the day; have moments in time.

— Douglas Pagels

FIND PLEASURE
IN LITTLE THINGS

Sing a song
Read a poem
Paint a picture
Dance to the music in your head
Rise up
and touch the stars —
today

— Susan Polis Schutz

Take the scenic route to work, find an exotic takeout restaurant to challenge your senses, or scout out a new spot to watch the sun set. Design a different pamper-yourself afternoon, read a whole new genre of books, learn about a foreign culture, or listen to a category of music you've never really explored before. Ask someone you'd like to meet to lunch, join a new chat room on the Internet, or call someone you love in the middle of the day. Take up yoga or meditation; join a cycling club or rowing crew. Run a marathon, build a birdhouse, or paint your front door red.

— Suzanne Willis Zoglio, Ph.D.

WAYS TO KEEP IT SIMPLE

Cultivate gratitude.
Carve out an hour a day for solitude.
Begin and end the day with prayer, meditation,
reflection.
Keep it simple.
Keep your house picked up.
Don't overschedule.
Strive for realistic deadlines.
Never make a promise you can't keep.
Allow an extra half hour for everything you do.
Create quiet surroundings at home and at work.
Go to bed at nine o'clock twice a week.
Always carry something interesting to read.
Breathe — deeply and often.
Move — walk, dance, run, find a sport you enjoy.
Drink pure spring water. Lots of it.
Eat only when hungry.
If it's not delicious, don't eat it.
Be instead of do.
Set aside one day a week for rest and renewal.
Laugh more often.
Luxuriate in your senses.
Always opt for comfort.
If you don't love it, live without it.

Let Mother Nature nurture.
Don't answer the telephone during dinner.
Stop trying to please everybody.
Start pleasing yourself.
Stay away from negative people.
Don't squander precious resources: time,
    creative energy, emotion.
Nurture friendships.
Don't be afraid of your passion.
Approach problems as challenges.
Honor your aspirations.
Set achievable goals.
Surrender expectations.
Savor beauty.
Create boundaries.
For every "yes," let there be a "no."
Don't worry; be happy.
Remember, happiness is a living emotion.
Exchange security for serenity.
Care for your soul.
Cherish your dreams.
Express love every day.
Search for your authentic self until you find her.

— *Sarah Ban Breathnach*

Take a Day Away from It All

Each person deserves a day away in which no problems are confronted, no solutions searched for. Each of us needs to withdraw from the cares which will not withdraw from us. We need hours of aimless wandering or spates of time sitting on park benches, observing the mysterious world of ants and the canopy of treetops. A day away acts as a spring tonic. It can dispel rancor, transform indecision, and renew the spirit.

— *Maya Angelou*

Rest is not idleness, and to lie sometimes on the grass under trees on a summer's day, listening to the murmur of the water, or watching the clouds float across the sky, is by no means a waste of time.

— *Sir J. Lubbock*

ENJOY THE WORLD AROUND YOU

The world was made
to be beautiful —
but sometimes we get caught up in
everyday actions
completely forgetting about this
completely forgetting that
what is truly important
are the simple, basic things in life —
honest, pure emotions
surrounded by the majestic beauty of nature
We need to concentrate on
the freeness and peacefulness of nature
and not on the driven material aspects of life
We need to smell the clear air
after the rainfall
and appreciate the good in things
Each of us must be responsible and do our part
in order to help preserve a beautiful world —
the waterfalls, the oceans, the mountains
the large gray boulders
the large green farms
the fluffy pink clouds
the sunrise and sunset, ladybugs
rainbows, dew, hummingbirds
butterflies, dandelions
We need to remember that
we are here for a short time
and that every day should count for something and
that every day we should be thankful
for all the natural beauty
The world is a wonderful place
and we are so lucky to be a part of it

— Susan Polis Schutz

Nature cannot heal and help us while we are rushing about. We must stop and relax if nature is to work her magic. There is little value in a hurried glance at a mountain brook, but to take off our shoes and socks and wade in the brook, or to sit on the bank and watch it for an hour, is to feel its peace and music flowing through us.

— Wilferd A. Peterson

I remember a hundred lovely lakes, and recall the fragrant breath of pine and fir and cedar and poplar trees. The trail has strung upon it, as upon a thread of silk, opalescent dawns and saffron sunsets. It has given me blessed release from care and worry and the troubled thinking of our modern day. It has been a return to the primitive and the peaceful.

Whenever the pressure of our complex city life thins my blood and benumbs my brain, I seek relief in the trail; and when I hear the coyote wailing to the yellow dawn, my cares fall from me — I am happy.

— Hamlin Garland

Retreat to Nature

If the noise of the city offend you, go
    afield, when you may, with the birds
    and the wild free life that troubles not;
The growing grain and the placid sky
    have a kind of voice, and though you
    are alone, the boundlessness of the
    universe is with you.

The dream of imperishable passions in
    old history, the love of mothers for
    children, and the love of children, born
    and unborn, and all love swarm in the
    soft air, speaking to the inner ear in
    the still language.

Go afield with the birds and the growing
    grain and the placid sky, and dream
    and forget, and you will see that you
    are changed when you awake and the
    gleams of the city peep in your twilight
    returning.

— Max Ehrmann

plant a flower...

Working in the garden... gives... a profound feeling of inner peace. Nothing here is in a hurry. There is no rush toward accomplishment, no blowing of trumpets. Here is the great mystery of life and growth. Everything is changing, growing, aiming at something, but silently, unboastfully, taking its time.

— Ruth Stout

take a walk...

A walk. The atmosphere incredibly pure — a warm, caressing gentleness in the sunshine — joy in one's whole being.... Forgotten impressions of childhood and youth came back to me — all those indescribable effects wrought by color, shadow, sunlight, green hedges, and songs of birds, upon the soul just opening to poetry. I became young again, wondering, and simple, as candor and ignorance are simple. I abandoned myself to life and to nature, and they cradled me with an infinite gentleness.

— Henri Amiel

fly a kite...

Flying kites... makes you feel free and joyous. As the wind takes hold of the kite, you can feel it on your body, gently rocking you back and forth. The sky quietly accepts you, surrounding you and protecting you. You become a child yourself and your spirit is set free.... Look at the clouds and share the stories they tell. Run with the wind, or roll on the ground. There are no rules, just freedom. You can't force a kite; you just have to accept where the winds take it.

— Judy Ford

climb a mountain...

Climb the mountains and get their good tidings. Nature's peace will flow into you as sunshine flows into trees. The winds will blow their own freshness into you, and the storms their energy, while cares will drip off like autumn leaves.

— John Muir

AWAKEN YOUR SENSES

We see the world. We touch the world. We taste the world. We smell the world. We hear the world. Our senses are how we get information about the world and enjoy what's been created on the physical plane. If we merge with our senses, we realize we are the world.

— Jonathan Kramer, Ph.D., and Diane Dunaway Kramer

Train yourself to see the details of your life the way a photographer looks for the details of a scene. But don't stop with what you see: use all your senses to become a connoisseur of events and details.... Don't keep your appreciation of details to yourself. Point out the wild strawberries barely visible in the grass, the gargoyles atop an otherwise nondescript apartment building, the way the air today smells like London after a rain. And surround yourself with people who understand the importance of a nearly unnoticeable item or interlude. Because society at large applauds the big, the noisy, and the obvious, it's helpful to have in your personal world others who value the small, the quiet, and the subtle. Someone once said, "God is in the details." So are most of the pleasures of life.

— Victoria Moran

Smell the scent of honeysuckle in the perfumed air that follows a spring rain. Listen for the gentle song of wrens and the sound of escalating winds. Watch the ballet of lightning bugs on a hot humid night or barn swallows in flight at dusk. Enjoy the taste of wild berries whether gathered fresh or bought at a local market. A radiant sunrise, a sultry sunset, hemlock branches laden with snow... what better gifts are there than these? See the beauty in all that's near and bring it closer to you. Stop and pick a roadside cluster of Queen Anne's Lace, sit where the winter sun streams through a window, or watch a chickadee build a nest for its young out of twigs and lime-green moss. Plant an orange seed in a little paper cup and watch it grow to a glossy green. Take pleasure in the simple riches that surround us all.

— Suzanne Willis Zoglio, Ph.D.

*N*urture your sense of smell. Let it come alive. Use its power to help you heal. A bundle of white sage burning in a seashell on the table. The wisp of cedar smoke from the fireplace. A cone of incense filling the air. Lavender oil in the bath. Drops of eucalyptus sprinkled in the shower, its penetrating aroma mingling with the steam. A vanilla candle on the nightstand next to your bed. The smell of a forest, fresh with rain. Ocean air, salty and damp. The rich sawdust smell of redwood. Comforting smells from childhood — bread baking in the oven, freshly baked chocolate cake on the counter, chicken frying in the pan. The smell of our favorite people, their hair, their clothes, their cologne.

— *Melody Beattie*

I who am blind can give one hint to those who see. Use your eyes as if tomorrow you will have been stricken blind. Hear the music of voices, the song of a bird, the mighty strains of an orchestra as if you would be stricken deaf tomorrow. Touch each object as if tomorrow your tactile sense would fail. Smell the perfume of flowers, taste with relish each morsel as if tomorrow you could never taste or smell again. Make the most of each sense. Glory in all the facts and pleasures and beauty which the world reveals to you.

— *Helen Keller*

SIMPLE GIFTS
WE EACH CAN GIVE

A pebble thrown into a still pond will not make a huge wave, but it will make a ripple, which then reverberates outward till it reaches the edge of the shore. Like pebbles, we too have such an effect. With six billion people on the planet, it may seem as if each life is infinitesimal in its meaning, yet each person is essential to the whole and each holds the potential for greatness. Significant and lasting changes don't require huge committees or mythical heroes. All that's required is love.

— Brian Luke Seaward, Ph.D.

So many people walk around with a meaningless life. They seem half-asleep, even when they're busy doing things they think are important. This is because they're chasing the wrong things. The way you get meaning into your life is to devote yourself to loving others, devote yourself to your community around you, and devote yourself to creating something that gives you purpose and meaning.

— Morrie Schwartz

Each of us has a few minutes a day or a few hours a week which we could donate to an old folks' home or a children's hospital ward. The elderly whose pillows we plump or whose water pitchers we refill may or may not thank us for our gift, but the gift is upholding the foundation of the universe. The children to whom we read simple stories may or may not show gratitude, but each boon we give strengthens the pillars of the world.

— Maya Angelou

A smile, a sharing of the joys of the sunrise and sunset, perhaps teaching a small child to ride a bike or fly a kite... these are what counts in a lifetime. The time taken to push a swing, help a neighbor, write a letter, send a card... the giving of ourselves in a way that money can never replace... these are the things that will always be remembered.

— Ruth Fishel

GIFTS OF LOVE

A simple little man he was,
His clothing worn and poor,
Doing his Christmas shopping
In a crowded ten cent store.

A shiny, new tin pan, three dishcloths,
Chosen with such care,
You knew that he had never owned
A penny he could spare.

A brave, gay paper lamp shade,
A yard of oilcloth, neat;
A wistful look at price tags
His few cents could not meet.

And then, on weary feet he turned
Where glittering nosegays lay,
And with his last few pennies
Bought a holiday bouquet.

"It's for my wife for Christmas —
She likes pretty things," he said.
I blinked — and could have sworn
I saw a halo 'round his head.

— Helen Lowrie Marshall

*The priceless gifts we give to each other
are not the ones wrapped
in fancy paper,
but the gifts we give when
we give of ourselves.
It is the love that we share.
It is the comfort we lend in times of need.
It is the moments we spend together
helping each other follow our dreams.
The most priceless gifts we can give
are the understanding and caring
that come from the heart.
And each and every one of us
has these gifts to offer...
through the gift of ourselves.*

— *Ben Daniels*

The Gift of a Smile

She smiled at a sorrowful stranger.
The smile seemed to make him feel better.
He remembered the past kindness of a friend
And wrote him a thank-you letter.
The friend was so pleased with the thank you
That he left a large tip after lunch.
The waitress, surprised by the size of the tip,
Bet the whole thing on a hunch.
The next day she picked up her winnings,
And gave part to a man on the street.
The man on the street was grateful;
For two days he'd had nothing to eat.
After he finished his dinner,
He left for his small dingy room.
He didn't know at that moment
That he might be facing his doom.
On the way he picked up a shivering puppy
And took him home to get warm.
The puppy was very grateful
To be in out of the storm.
That night the house caught on fire.
The puppy barked the alarm.
He barked till he woke the whole household
And saved everybody from harm.
One of the boys that he rescued
Grew up to be President.
All this because of a simple smile.

— *Anonymous*

A smile costs nothing in money, time, or effort, but it is literally true that it can be of supreme importance in one's life. A smile affects your whole body from the skin right in to the skeleton, including all blood vessels, nerves and muscles. It affects the functioning of every organ. It influences every gland. I repeat — and this is literally true — you cannot smile without affecting your whole body favorably. Even one smile often relaxes quite a number of muscles, and when the thing becomes a habit you can easily see how the effect will mount up. *Last year's smiles are paying you dividends today.*

— Emmet Fox

Be happy in the moment, that's enough. Each moment is all we need, not more. Be happy now and if you show through your actions that you love others, including those who are poorer than you, you'll give them happiness, too. It doesn't take much — it can be just giving a smile. The world would be a much better place if everyone smiled more.

— Mother Teresa

Smile at someone only for the very important reason that every act of kindness is another chance to make this life experience a better one. A simple smile to someone you've never met may soften them, and perhaps the next opportunity they have to smile at a stranger they will do so, because they will remember the good feeling.

— Suzanne Somers

Simply Relax

We need to learn how to relax, how to unwind.

Find something that's relaxing, healing, soothing, and available to you. Sit in the sun. Sit in the tub. Take a trip to a nearby hot spring or mineral bath in your state. Perch atop a mountain or hill, taking in the view from above.

Let yourself sit and soak it in for as long as you can. Let yourself be still for as long as you can. Move around a bit if you need to. Then go back and try again.

Don't just do it once. Try it often. Allow yourself to relax. Give yourself opportunities to unwind. Soon you'll learn how.

Pay attention to what you think and feel when you try to relax. Watch, as a neutral observer, without judgment or reproach. What thoughts come to mind? How do you feel? What do you feel?

Go as deeply into your thoughts and feelings as you are able. Sit quietly for as long as you can. When your body is done, it will tell you.

— *Melody Beattie*

take a nap...

A nap is not to be confused with sleeping. We sleep to recharge our bodies. We nap to care for our souls. When we nap, we are resting our eyes while our imaginations soar. Getting ready for the next round. Sorting, sifting, separating the profound from the profane, the possible from the improbable. Rehearsing our acceptance speech for the Nobel Prize, our surprise on receiving the MacArthur genius award. This requires a prone position. If we're lucky, we might drift off, but we won't drift far. Just far enough to ransom our creativity from chaos.

— Sarah Ban Breathnach

read a book...

Books provide the perfect escape, allowing us to move beyond our daily stresses and find comfort in a world distant from our own. They allow us to transform into anyone we want to be and go anywhere we want to go. There is a great joy to be found in reading books, one that is unlike anything else.

— Deana Marino

visit a museum...

Stroll through a museum with nothing on your mind. Find a painting or sculpture that touches something in your heart. Sit down in front of it and look. Just look. Don't try to analyze. Just look. Let it overwhelm you. Drink it all in until you are full. Don't try to figure it out. Just look at all the details and the whole piece of art. Let the colors and textures swim into your mind. Let the art nourish your soul in secret ways, ways you can't begin to think about. Just look.

— Mitch Finley

take a bath...

When you are in the bathtub, you are not responsible for anything — you are wet, for example, so no one can ask you to do anything... you can't do work in there, because your papers will get wet... you can't answer the phone... or read any e-mail... or assignments... or messages... or...

...maybe it should be
a long bath.

— Ashley Rice

Refresh in Solitude

Settle into yourself
Be truly alone

And not the kind of alone
that makes your heart sore
but the kind that causes
your breath to slow
your limbs to go weightless
your thoughts to fall from you
one by one

Embrace the moment
that leaves you in
complete solitude
Welcome these times
as a gift of peace
for your spirit and soul

Your sustenance

— Elle Mastro

MAKE TIME FOR YOU

At any given moment on any given day, you
are needed. Needed to talk... to drive... to sing...
to dance... to laugh... to listen... to help... to
walk... to do... something. You say you'll make
time for you when things slow down, but things
will never slow down unless you allow them to.

There will always be that something waving in
the background relentlessly trying to get your
attention. It's up to you to turn your back... shut
your eyes... walk in the opposite direction of that
something that just refuses to give you a break.
Take the time you deserve to check in with
yourself and see what you need for a change.

Be completely and utterly selfish, and by no means
let guilt creep into your sacred space. No, it's not
easy, which is why you have to commit to making
a conscious effort to concentrate solely on you
and your needs. Say no. Unplug your phone.
Lock your door to the world. Do whatever it takes
to make no one but you the ultimate priority.

— Elle Mastro

You must have a room, or a certain hour or so a day, where you don't know what was in the newspapers that morning, you don't know who your friends are, you don't know what you owe anybody, you don't know what anybody owes to you. This is a place where you can simply experience and bring forth what you are and what you might be.

— Joseph Campbell

It is a difficult lesson to learn today — to leave one's friends and family and deliberately practice the art of solitude for an hour or a day or a week.... And yet, once it is done, I find there is a quality to being alone that is incredibly precious. Life rushes back into the void, richer, more vivid, fuller than before.

— Anne Morrow Lindbergh

The World Is a Magical Place

The rabbit in the hat once empty, the fairy
dust that makes white doves appear, the
nothing that turns into something spectacular,
the mind reader that guesses your hidden
card, the men that fly, the lady that splits in
two yet remains unharmed...

these are mere mysteries.

But the butterfly that dances near the sun,
the child that walks his very first steps, the
colors that appear after the rain, the shapes
of dinosaurs and castles formed in the clouds,
the trail of light left behind by a falling star,
the sound of leaves rustling, the tiny buds
that grow into brilliant yellow roses...

these are magic.

— Elle Mastro

Centuries-old trees, trees covered with mossy hair, shared their stories with me. Felled trees lying on their backs beckoned me to touch, to sit, to rest a while. Sunlight glistened through the entangled underbrush. The air smelled of nature's sawdust. The ground was warm, moist. Nature sprites danced and played along the path. The birds serenaded me with calls, whistles, and songs, like sounds emanating from a flute. Magic was in the air.

— *Melody Beattie*

If no one had ever seen a flower, even a dandelion would be the most startling event in the world.

— *Anonymous*

We were talking about magic
as we drove along a crowded
Sunday highway

when the whir of wings
made me turn
and a flock of geese

flew over our car
so low I could see
their feet tucked under them.

For a moment the rustle
of their presence over our heads
obscured everything

and as they disappeared
you said,
"I see what you mean."

— Jenifer Nostrand

Discover the Child
Within You

Release the child within you
so you can sing,
laugh, and play.
List the things
that you do best,
and give yourself a hug.
Accept compliments.
Dance barefoot.
Plan to fulfill a secret wish.
Laugh at yourself.
And above all,
remember you are loved.

— Jacqueline Schiff

We need to find the strength and hope
   from our childhood
We need to forgive and laugh again
We need to remember life through a child's eyes
And let it carry us through our life

— Susan Mah

Know you what it is to be a child?...
It is to believe in love, to believe in
loveliness, to believe in beliefs; it is
to be so little that the elves can reach
to whisper in your ear; it is to turn
pumpkins into coaches, and mice into
horses, lowness into loftiness, and
nothing into everything, for each
child has its fairy godmother in its
own soul.

— Francis Thompson

When a little boy on his scooter hit a bump in the sidewalk and took a tumble, he paused and then burst out laughing.

A passer-by who saw no fun in the bruises asked: "What's so funny? Why laugh about it?"

The boy replied, "Mister, I'm laughing so I won't cry."

— Leroy Brownlow

∴⌐

Breathe life back into your imagination. Come back to life. Let yourself see dragons in clouds and leprechauns in trees and velvet in a rose. Imagine what it would be like to grab a handful of cloud. Then touch the tree. And put the rose to your cheek.

— Melody Beattie

Laughter Lightens the Heart

There is one kind of laugh that I always did recommend; it looks out of the eye first with a merry twinkle, then it creeps down on its hands and knees and plays around the mouth like a pretty moth around the blaze of a candle, then it steals over into the dimples of the cheeks and rides around in those whirlpools for a while, then it lights up the whole face like the mellow bloom on a damask rose, then it swims up on the air, with a peal as clear and as happy as a dinner-bell, then it goes back again on gold tiptoes like an angel out for an airing, and it lies down on its little bed of violets in the heart where it came from.

— Josh Billings

*Cherish the gift of humor. Life doesn't
need to be so gloomy. Spirituality doesn't
need to be so serious and somber. Work
doesn't need to be that way either. Learn to
see the humor in life. Look for it. Find it.
Enjoy it. Surround yourself with people who
like to laugh. Being around people who
laugh can open us up to the power of humor
in our own lives. Laughter can become
contagious. There is something magnetic,
something healing, about being around
people who let themselves laugh often.*

— *Melody Beattie*

*Always laugh when you can; it is cheap medicine.
Merriment is a philosophy not well understood.
It's the sunny side of existence.*

— *George Gordon, Lord Byron*

Laughter reminds you that... daily incidents are unimportant and not worth getting worked up about. Laughter is God's tranquilizer. Laughter calms the soul and releases endorphins, which are the feel-good hormones. Use laughter as your inner therapist. Little things won't overwhelm you unnecessarily when you can laugh about them.

— Suzanne Somers

You know. You remember the sound of it. It's what kids do in the back seat of a car with their friends. It's the sound that wafts down from the bedroom when the door is closed and they think no one can hear them.... Mostly, though, it's about the sheer joy of being alive. It's about absolutely nothing in particular and everything specific that has made its way into the appreciation of this particular moment in time. Right here. Right now.

— Elizabeth Kaeton

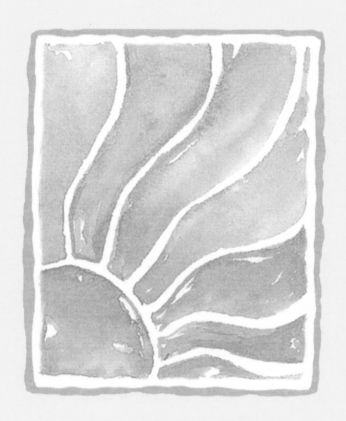

Searching for the Simple Life

Take one moment at a time.
Hear music.
Make music.
Seek inspiration.
Learn.
Believe in fairy tales
and in the magic
of your dreams.
Find that dreams do come true.
Hug yourself.
Feel the sun shine.
Believe again.
Smile.
Seek laughter.
Always remember that you have
a guardian angel
watching over you.
Be kind to yourself.
Look in the mirror and see
that you are beautiful.
Make three wishes.
Be strong.
Nurture your soul.

— Linda Ann McConnell

Simplicity looks different in different lives because each heart holds its own themes. It looks different at different times of our own lives because our tempos change with age, events, and experience.

Simplicity is not a matter of time management or efficiency or organization. It does not consist of shedding one set of life furnishings in order to make room for another. Rather, a simpler life is one in which the knowledge of what matters dictates all that surrounds us. It is a life lived with the courage to let go of what our hearts know does not belong. It is a more balanced life, not a more expert balancing act....

There is no right or wrong in the search for simplicity. It is not a destination, like a house we move into, but a direction, like the path that leads toward the house. Where it takes us, if we dare to follow, is back to our hearts.

— *Andrea Van Steenhouse, Ph.D.*

Simplifying is not necessarily about getting rid of everything we've worked so hard for. It's about making wise choices among the things we now have to choose from. It's about recognizing that trying to have it all has gotten in the way of enjoying the things which do add to our happiness and well-being. So it's about deciding what's important to us, and gracefully letting go of the things that aren't.

An amazing thing happens when we slow down. We start to get flashes of inspiration. We reach a new level of understanding and even wisdom. In a quiet moment we can get an intuitive insight that can change our entire life and the lives of the people around us in incredibly positive ways. And those changes can last a lifetime.

Living more simply will make it possible to create those quiet moments. Out of those quiet moments miracles happen. Be open to them.

— *Elaine St. James*

Take Nothing for Granted

Take nothing for granted: the sheer act
of waking each day; fresh air upon your cheek;
each effort expended on self or another —
walking the dog, shopping for food, toiling
at home   in an office   or on the road.
Every moment is rare, short, and full of glory.
Every word is magic; a story achieved through
    will.
Marvel at nature's moods as mirror of your own.
Recall a sunrise or sunset, a flock of geese in the
    sky.
Care about parents or children as fragile gifts
like petal on a rose, like song from one bird.
Praise the simple or complex — the invention of
    flight
above clouds; the wheel; the bathtub; a rocking-
    chair.
We rise and fall in the moon or a wave,
in a smile or many tears. And being brave
is to be alive as we give and share love
always, only and ever to survive.

— Rochelle Lynn Holt

BELIEVE IN MIRACLES

Live this day well.
Let a little sunshine out as well as in.
Create your own rainbows.
Be open to all your possibilities;
*   possibilities can be miracles.*
Always believe in miracles!

— *Vickie M. Worsham*

It was Einstein who said
either nothing is a miracle,
or everything is —
a jagged mountain range,
lilacs in bloom,
a peacock unfurled,
sun on your arm,
the touch of a stranger.

Take your pick: be surprised
by nothing at all,
or by everything that is.

— *Maryanne Hannan*

Look around you.
Open your eyes and
let yourself be amazed
by life itself.
Open your mind and heart
and observe.
Notice.
Notice everything.

Wake up to the miracles.
They're everywhere.
In the sunrise, the sunset,
a breath, a flower.
Behold your hands and feet,
how they serve you.
What miracles!
Everywhere.

You are surrounded by
these acts of God.
You, yourself, are one of these.
Just be aware of their presence
and, like a new miracle,
all numbness and emptiness
are transformed into reverence
and the joy of being alive.

— *Phylis Clay Sparks*

Most of All... Be Happy

Always see the goodness in this world,
do your part in helping those
 less fortunate,
walk hand in hand with those
 of less talent,
follow those of more knowledge,
and be an equal with those who
 are different.
Find your special purpose in this world
 so full of choices
and help lead those who stray.
Become your own individual —
set yourself apart from those who
 are the same.
Have the self-confidence to say no
when it is necessary and the strength
 to stand alone.
Give yourself the approval to love
and respect everything that you are
 and will become.
Reap the fruits of your talents,
walk with pride down the road of life,
be humble in your successes,
and share in the praises and joy of others.

 Most of all...
  be happy.

       — Jackie Olson

ACKNOWLEDGMENTS

We gratefully acknowledge the permission granted by the following authors, publishers, and authors' representatives to reprint poems or excerpts from their publications.

The Brownlow Corporation for "It's the little things..." and "When a little boy..." from TODAY IS MINE by Leroy Brownlow. Copyright © 1972 by Leroy Brownlow. All rights reserved.

PrimaDonna Entertainment Corp., for "Make every day a day to..." and "See each day as a new opportunity..." by Donna Fargo. Copyright © 1998, 2000 by PrimaDonna Entertainment Corp. All rights reserved.

Tower Hill Press for "Take the scenic route..." and "Smell the scent..." from CREATE A LIFE THAT TICKLES YOUR SOUL by Suzanne Willis Zoglio, Ph.D. Copyright © 1999 by Suzanne Willis Zoglio, Ph.D. All rights reserved.

Warner Books, Inc., for "Cultivate gratitude..." and "A nap is not..." from SIMPLE ABUNDANCE by Sarah Ban Breathnach. Copyright © 1995 by Sarah Ban Breathnach. All rights reserved.

Random House Inc., and Virago Press for "Each person deserves..." and "Each of us has..." from WOULDN'T TAKE NOTHING FOR MY JOURNEY NOW by Maya Angelou. Copyright © 1993 by Maya Angelou. All rights reserved.

Heacock Literary Agency, Inc., for "Nature cannot heal and help..." from THE ART OF LIVING, DAY BY DAY by Wilferd A. Peterson, published by Simon & Schuster, Inc. Copyright © 1972 by Wilferd A. Peterson. All rights reserved.

Crown Publishers, a division of Random House, Inc., for "If the Noise of the City" from THE DESIDERATA OF HOPE by Max Ehrmann. Copyright 1948 by Bertha K. Ehrmann. Copyright © renewed 1976 by Robert L. Bell. All rights reserved. And for "Smile at someone..." and "Laughter reminds you..." from 365 WAYS TO CHANGE YOUR LIFE by Suzanne Somers. Copyright © 1999 by Suzanne Somers. All rights reserved. And for "Simplicity looks different..." from A WOMAN'S GUIDE TO A SIMPLER LIFE by Andrea Van Steenhouse, Ph.D. Copyright © 1996 by Andrea Van Steenhouse, Ph.D. and Doris A. Fuller. All rights reserved.

Childreach, on behalf of Ruth Stout, for "Working in the garden..." from HOW TO HAVE A GREEN THUMB WITHOUT AN ACHING BACK by Ruth Stout, published by Exposition-Phoenix Press. Copyright © 1955 by Ruth Stout. All rights reserved.

Conari Press, an imprint of Red Wheel/Weiser, for "Flying kites..." from WONDERFUL WAYS TO LOVE A CHILD by Judy Ford. Copyright © 1944 by Judy Ford. All rights reserved. And for "A pebble thrown into..." from STRESSED IS DESSERTS SPELLED BACKWARDS by Brian Luke Seaward, Ph.D. Copyright © 1999 by Brian Luke Seaward, Ph.D. All rights reserved.

Doubleday, a division of Random House, Inc., and Loretta Barrett Books for "We see the world..." from LOSING THE WEIGHT OF THE WORLD by Jonathan Kramer, Ph.D. and Diane Kramer. Copyright © 1997 by Jonathan Kramer and Diane Kramer. All rights reserved.

HarperCollins Publishers for "Train yourself to see..." from CREATING A CHARMED LIFE by Victoria Moran. Copyright © 1999 by Victoria Moran. All rights reserved. And for "Nurture your sense...," "We need to learn...," "Centuries-old trees...," "Breathe life back...," and "Cherish the gift..." from JOURNEY TO THE HEART: DAILY MEDITATIONS ON THE PATH TO FREEING YOUR SOUL by Melody Beattie. Copyright © 1996 by Melody Beattie. All rights reserved. And for "A smile costs nothing in money..." from MAKE YOUR LIFE WORTH WHILE by Emmet Fox. Copyright 1942, 1943, 1944, 1945, 1946 by Emmet Fox. Copyright renewed © 1974 by Kathleen Whelan. All rights reserved.

American Foundation for the Blind Press for "I who am blind" from TO LOVE THIS LIFE: QUOTATIONS by Helen Keller. Copyright © 2000 by the American Foundation for the Blind. All rights reserved.

Doubleday, a division of Random House, Inc., and Black, Inc., for "So many people walk around..." by Morrie Schwartz from TUESDAYS WITH MORRIE by Mitch Albom. Copyright © 1997 by Mitch Albom. All rights reserved.

Health Communications, Inc., for "A smile, a sharing..." from TIME FOR JOY by Ruth Fishel. Copyright © 1988 by Ruth Fishel. All rights reserved.

"A simple little man..." from CLOSE TO THE HEART by Helen Lowrie Marshall. Copyright © 1958 by Helen Lowrie Marshall.

Ballantine Books, a division of Random House, Inc., and The Random House Group Limited for "Be happy in the moment..." from A SIMPLE PATH by Mother Teresa, edited by Lucinda Vardey. Copyright © 1995 by Lucinda Vardey. All rights reserved.

The Crossroad Publishing Company for "Stroll through a museum..." from 101 WAYS TO NOURISH YOUR SOUL by Mitch Finley. Copyright © 1996 by Mitch Finley. All rights reserved.

Doubleday, a division of Random House, Inc., for "You must have..." from THE POWER OF MYTH by Joseph Campbell & Bill Moyers. Copyright © 1988 by Apostrophe S Productions, Inc., and Bill Moyers and Alfred Van der Marck Editions, Inc. for itself and the estate of Joseph Campbell. All rights reserved.

Pantheon Books, a division of Random House, Inc., for "It is a difficult lesson..." from GIFT FROM THE SEA by Anne Morrow Lindbergh. Copyright © 1955 by Anne Morrow Lindbergh. All rights reserved.

Jenifer Nostrand for "We were talking about magic...." Copyright © 1998 by Jenifer Nostrand. All rights reserved.

Susan Mah for "We need to find the strength...." Copyright © 2003 by Susan Mah. All rights reserved.

The Diocese of Newark for "You know. You remember..." from "Giggle Theory" by Elizabeth Kaeton in The Voice (June 2000). Copyright © 2000 by The Voice. All rights reserved.

Linda Ann McConnell for "Take one moment at a time." Copyright © 2003 by Linda Ann McConnell. All rights reserved.

Hyperion for "Simplifying is not..." and "An amazing thing happens..." from LIVING THE SIMPLE LIFE by Elaine St. James. Copyright © 1996 by Elaine St. James. All rights reserved.

Rochelle Lynn Holt for "Take Nothing for Granted." Copyright © 1998 by Rochelle Lynn Holt. All rights reserved.

Maryanne Hannan for "Epiphany" from BLESS THE DAY, by June Cotner. Copyright © 1998 by June Cotner, published by Kodashna International. Reprinted with permission from the author. All rights reserved.

Phylis Clay Sparks for "Look around you...." Copyright © 2003 by Phylis Clay Sparks. All rights reserved.

A careful effort has been made to trace the ownership of selections used in this anthology in order to obtain permission to reprint copyrighted material and give proper credit to the copyright owners. If any error or omission has occurred, it is completely inadvertent, and we would like to make corrections in future editions provided that written notification is made to the publisher:

BLUE MOUNTAIN ARTS, INC., P.O. Box 4549, Boulder, Colorado 80306.